1/03

Palo Alto City Library

The individual borrower is responsible for all library material borrowed on his or her card.

Charges as determined by the CITY OF PALO ALTO will be assessed for each overdue item.

Damaged or non-returned property will be billed to the individual borrower by the CITY OF PALO ALTO.

P.O. Box 10250, Palo Alto, CA 94303

The 3-D Library of the Human Body

THE STOMACH
LEARNING HOW
WE DIGEST

James Toriello

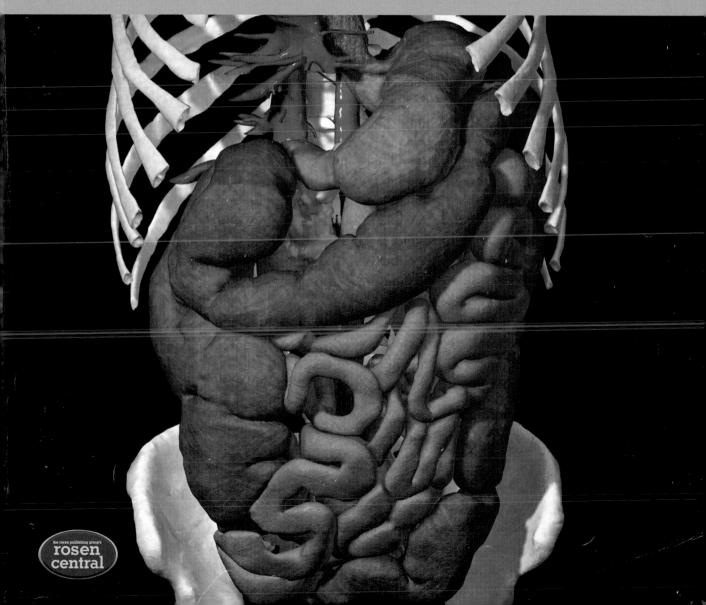

the rosen publishing group's
rosen
central

Editor's Note

The idea for the illustrations in this book originated in 1986 with the Vesalius Project at Colorado State University's Department of Anatomy and Neurobiology. There, a team of scientists and illustrators dreamed of turning conventional two-dimensional anatomical illustrations into three-dimensional computer images that could be rotated and viewed from any angle, for the benefit of students of medicine and biology. In 1988 this dream became the Visible Human Project™, under the sponsorship of the National Library of Medicine in Bethesda, Maryland. A grant was awarded to the University of Colorado School of Medicine, and in 1993 the first work of dissection and scanning began on the body of a Texas convict who had been executed by lethal injection. The process was repeated on the body of a Maryland woman who had died of a heart attack. Applying the latest techniques of computer graphics, the scientific team was able to create a series of three-dimensional digital images of the human body so beautiful and startlingly accurate that they seem more in the realm of art than science. On the computer screen, muscles, bones, and organs of the body can be turned and viewed from any angle, and layers of tissue can be electronically peeled away to reveal what lies underneath. In reproducing these digital images in two-dimensional print form, the editors at Rosen have tried to preserve the three-dimensional character of the work by showing organs of the body from different perspectives and using illustrations that progressively reveal deeper layers of anatomical structure.

Published in 2002 by The Rosen Publishing Group, Inc.
29 East 21st Street, New York, NY 10010

Digital anatomy images published by arrangement with Anatographica, LLC.
216 East 49th Street, New York, NY 10017

First Edition

Library of Congress Cataloging-in-Publication Data

Toriello, James.
The stomach: learning how we digest / James Toriello. — 1st ed.
p. cm. — (The 3-D library of the human body)
Includes bibliographical references and index.
Summary: A discussion of the anatomy of the stomach and abdomen and how we digest our food.
ISBN 0-8239-3536-1
1. Stomach—Juvenile literature. 2. Digestion—Juvenile literature. [1. Stomach. 2. Digestion. 3. Digestive system.]
I. Title. II. Series.
QP151 .T67 2001
612.3'2—dc21
                                                                                    2001002887

Manufactured in the United States of America

CONTENTS

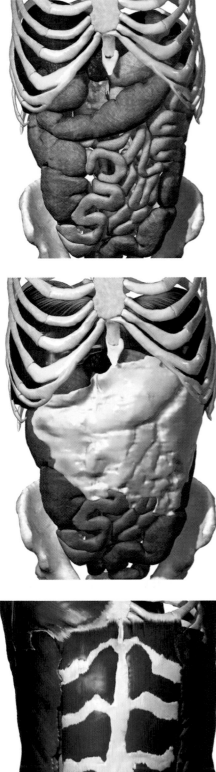

PREFACE
THE BODY SNATCHERS

Our understanding of human anatomy would never have been possible without the willingness of doctors and surgeons to perform dissections of human corpses. But throughout history, this has been easier said than done. Moral and religious prohibitions against the dismemberment of cadavers had for centuries created a shortage of dead bodies. The Greeks and Romans forbade the dissection of human beings, and the ancient Greek physician Galen had to draw conclusions about human anatomy from the dissection of pigs and monkeys. In later times, the Catholic Church forbade dissections, and like the furor over abortion today, the rumor that dissections were being performed could produce public demonstrations and riots. Even the great seventeenth-century physician William Harvey, who discovered the circulation of the blood, dissected his own father and sister for the lack of a plentiful source of dead bodies.

Yet dissections were being performed, hundreds of them a year in the anatomy schools of London alone. Laws allowed for the dissection of some hanged criminals, but that couldn't explain all the dissections. The public was rightly convinced that doctors were paying professional grave robbers to dig up corpses. It was not difficult to rob the graves of the poor, who were often buried together in large pits without coffins. In 1721, the Edinburgh College of Surgeons had to forbid its medical students from involvement in exhumation. There was also a widespread suspicion that, with the demand for bodies so great, some of the bodies supplied to doctors were not dead when they were snatched. There was the famous case of two Edinburgh cobblers, William Burke and William Hare, who sold bodies to the medical school of Dr. Robert Knox. When one of the tenants at Hare's lodging house got drunk and fell ill, the two men smothered her and sold her body to Dr. Knox for ten pounds. Fifteen more cadavers were supplied under suspicious circumstances. When they were discovered, Hare provided evidence against Burke to save himself, and Burke was executed in 1829. His body, ironically, was given to Dr. Knox's school for dissection.

In 1832, in Aberdeen, Scotland, 20,000 people rioted and burned down a medical school when human remains were discovered there. This lead to Parliament's passage of the Anatomy Act in the same year. Now anyone applying for free treatment at a hospital, or anyone supported by the state in a workhouse, was considered to have granted permission for the medical use of his or her body upon death. Again, the burden fell mostly on the poor, because hospitals at this time were for those who couldn't afford private doctors.

The shortage of bodies for medical schools continued into the 1920s, when moral prejudices began to fade and more and more people began to donate their bodies to medical science. The era of the body snatcher came to an end.

1
THE ABDOMEN

We often call the middle part of our body the stomach, but our midsection, or abdomen, actually contains many other vital organs. The midsection houses almost the entire digestive system, our body's food factory and energy distribution center. The abdomen, or trunk, also contains powerful muscles and important bones. These connect the upper and lower body and provide a safe place for digestion to take place.

Like other areas of the body, the abdomen also includes blood vessels, which ferry nutrients to needy cells and organs. The nerves in the trunk communicate sensations to the brain and send directions to muscles. And the lymph vessels help fight bodily intruders, an important consideration for the digestive organs.

Skin and Muscles

As in other parts of the body, the skin of the body's midsection covers a layer of fat. There are two parts to this layer. The outer layer can be thick or thin, depending on a person's weight. In fact, this is the part most of us pinch when we're trying to see if we're overweight or not.

The outer layer of fat is known as Camper's fascia. The word "fascia" is taken from the Latin word for bandage or girdle. It is used in anatomy and medicine to describe body tissues that bind structures

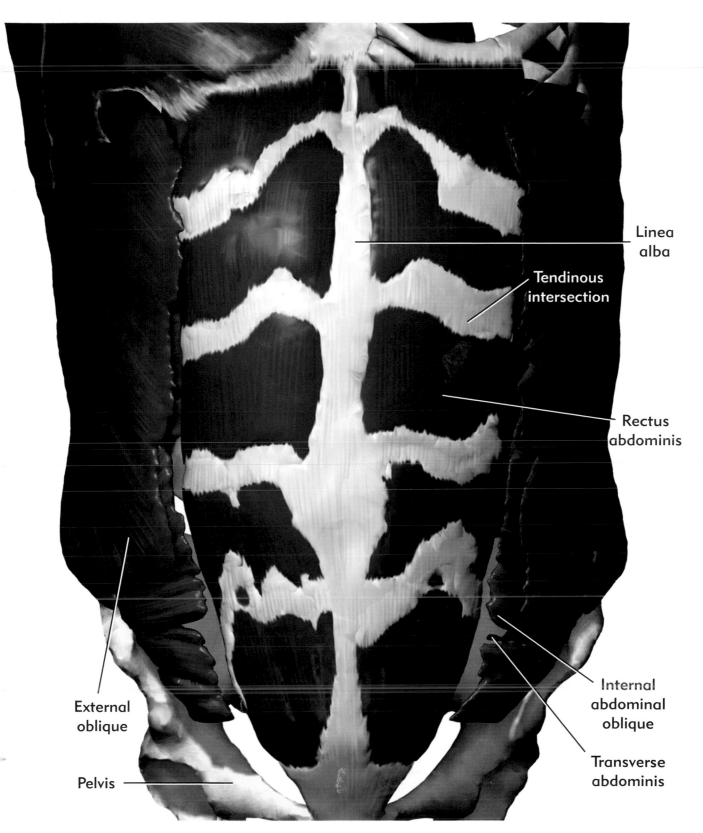

Linea alba

Tendinous intersection

Rectus abdominis

Internal abdominal oblique

Transverse abdominis

External oblique

Pelvis

No bones enclose and protect the abdomen. Instead, four paired, flat muscles and their tendons cover the underlying organs. Theses muscles help to flex and rotate the trunk of the body.

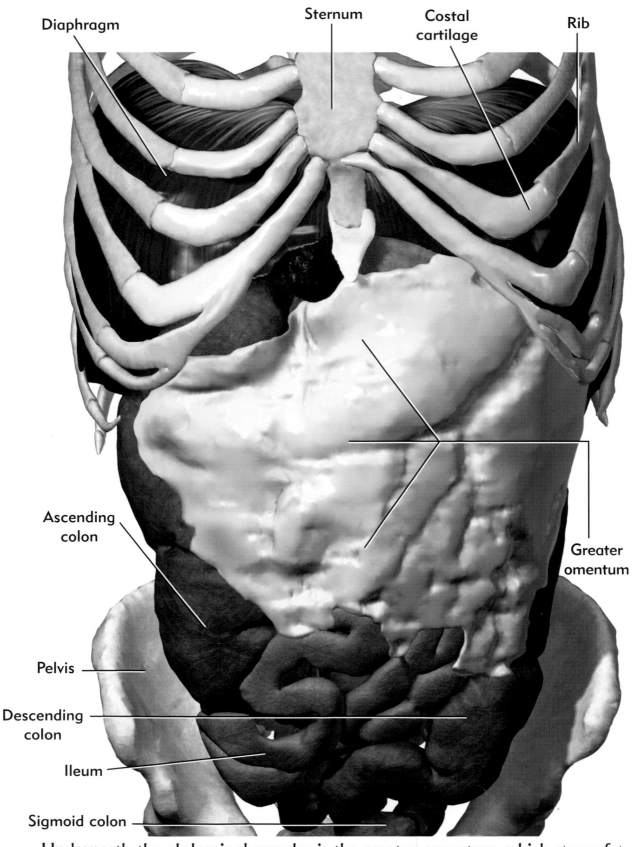

Diaphragm

Sternum

Costal
cartilage

Rib

Ascending
colon

Pelvis

Descending
colon

Ileum

Sigmoid colon

Greater
omentum

Underneath the abdominal muscles is the greater omentum, which stores fat
and helps to anchor the digestive organs to the abdominal wall.

together. Camper's fascia is named for early Dutch physician and scientist Pieter Camper, who lived in the eighteenth century. Today, Camper is best known for discovering that birds' bones have air spaces in them.

Bodybuilders are often admired for their shapely abdominal muscles. The shape comes from a number of interwoven muscles. They're not just for show; they give the abdomen flexibility and help to protect and hold the interior organs together. They also assist the diaphragm during breathing and help in the body's elimination of waste. When women give birth, the abdominal muscles help push the baby into the world.

Five main muscles make up the abdominal wall. Three are flat. They compress and support the trunk of the body. They run almost like bandages wrapped in slightly different directions around the midsection. They are the external oblique, internal oblique, and traverse abdominal muscles. A mirror image of each muscle extends around each side to the center of the body. These halves lace together at the linea alba, Latin for "white line," which is what the thick sheet of tendons at the end of the muscles looks like.

The linea alba contains small blood vessels and nerves, which run out to the skin. It also has an unusual hole: the navel. This is all that remains of the umbilical cord that connected the developing fetus to its mother before birth.

The external oblique muscles are the largest of the three muscles. The muscle fibers mostly run at a diagonal from back to front, or "inferomedially" as students of anatomy say. If you place your hands in your pants pockets with your thumbs sticking out, the direction of your fingers will be in roughly the same direction as the muscle fibers. The internal oblique muscles form the next layer, fanning out from about the hip. The traverse muscles form the inner layer. These traverse, or go around, the midsection.

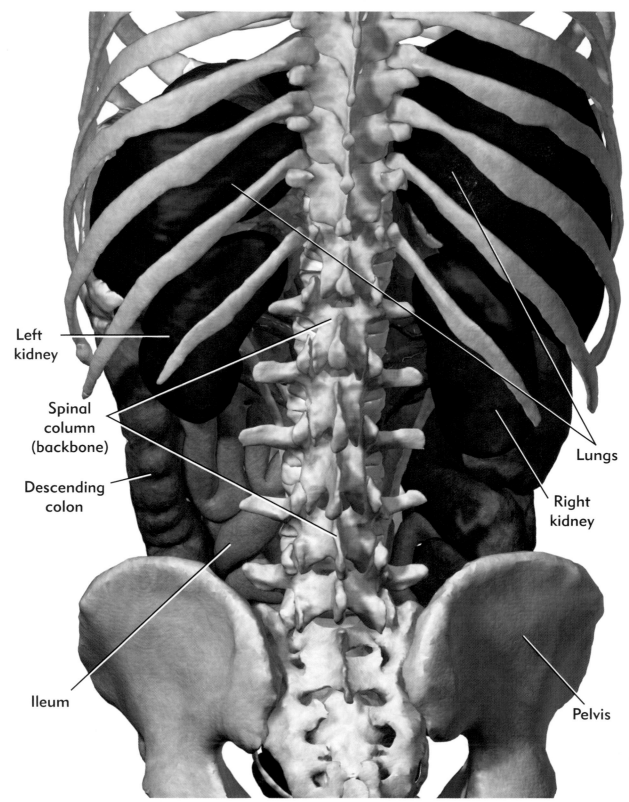

Left
kidney

Spinal
column
(backbone)

Descending
colon

Ileum

Lungs

Right
kidney

Pelvis

A posterior (rear) view of the abdominal area. The abdominal organs lie
above the pelvis, in front of the backbone and kidneys.

The rectus abdominis and pyramidalis are vertical muscles. They help flex the trunk of the body. If you've ever done a sit-up or even just bent over, you were putting them to work.

Three or more sections of the rectus abdominis line up in pairs down the front of the body. These sections are connected by thick tendons. When a bodybuilder tenses these muscles, the abdomen seems to bulge with a series of ripples or steps. The overall shape is often compared to a washboard.

Surprisingly, 20 percent of humans do not have the pyramidalis, a small triangular-shaped muscle near the pubic area at the base of the rectus abdominis. This muscle tenses the linea alba at the very bottom of the abdominal wall.

The Spinal Cord, Pelvis, and Ribs

Below the skin and muscles, bones shape the body. The lower ribs and pelvic bones cradle the midsection. The backbone, also known as the vertebral or spinal column, joins them together.

The Language of Anatomy

Many anatomical terms come from Latin and Greek words. There are many reasons. Western medicine dates to Greek and Roman times. Latin was the common language in Europe during the Roman Empire. Doctors spoke it and used it to describe body parts and medical concepts. After the fall of Rome, Latin remained a common language of learning. Students and teachers used it to communicate even if they came from different places. Their texts were also written in Latin. Since the human body hasn't changed during historical times, there has been no real need to invent new names.

The vertebral column protects the spinal cord and spinal nerves, which are like telephone lines or computer wires connecting the brain with the rest of the body. The spine also helps support and balance a person as he or she stands, sits, and moves. Overall, there are thirty-three vertebrae, or small bones, joined by discs in the spinal column.

The vertebrae interlock like the pieces of a bicycle chain. Bony wings face the back and sides of the body. The discs between the bones work like tiny rubber washers between these connections, giving the back some flexibility. Muscles along the column add strength and stability.

Rib bones fan out from the spinal column to the front of the body. Without skin, muscle, and internal organs, the ribs look a little like a birdcage or the framework of an unfinished building. This cage encloses the chest and abdomen, shaping the body and protecting the internal organs.

The ribs veer upward in the front of the body, forming a V on each side. This leaves the stomach and other internal organs room to expand in the front of the body. Every time you have a big meal, you take advantage of this space. It also gives surgeons easy access if they have to operate here.

The pelvis forms the base of the body's midsection. This strong collection of bones transfers weight from the upper body to the legs. Four bones do the job here: the two hip bones, the sacrum, and the coccyx. These bony structures are slightly different in men and women. In general, women's pelvic bones provide a wide opening to be used for birth. Male or female, the pelvic cavity contains the bladder, the rectum, and the genital organs.

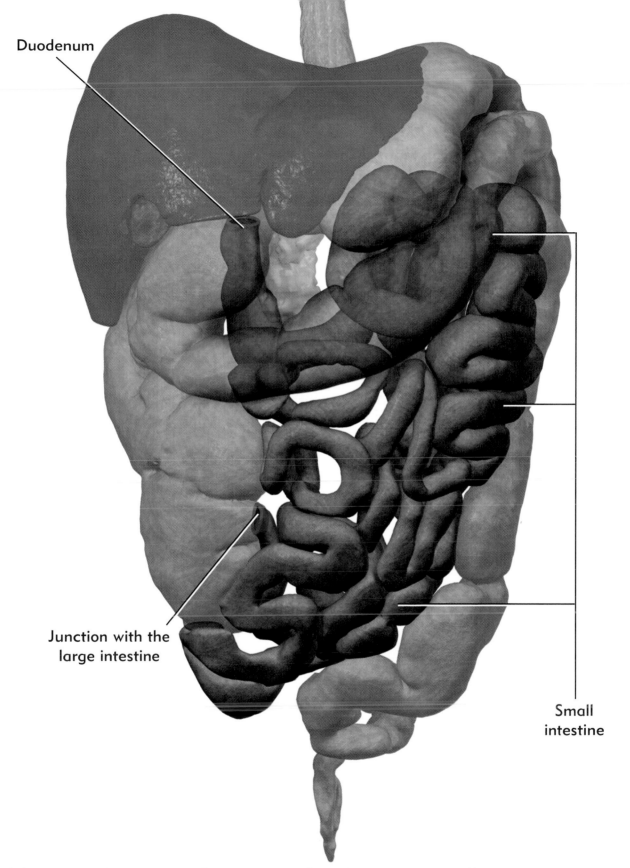

Duodenum

Junction with the
large intestine

Small
intestine

More than 99 percent of digestion takes place in the small intestine.
Nutrients are absorbed into the bloodstream through its walls.

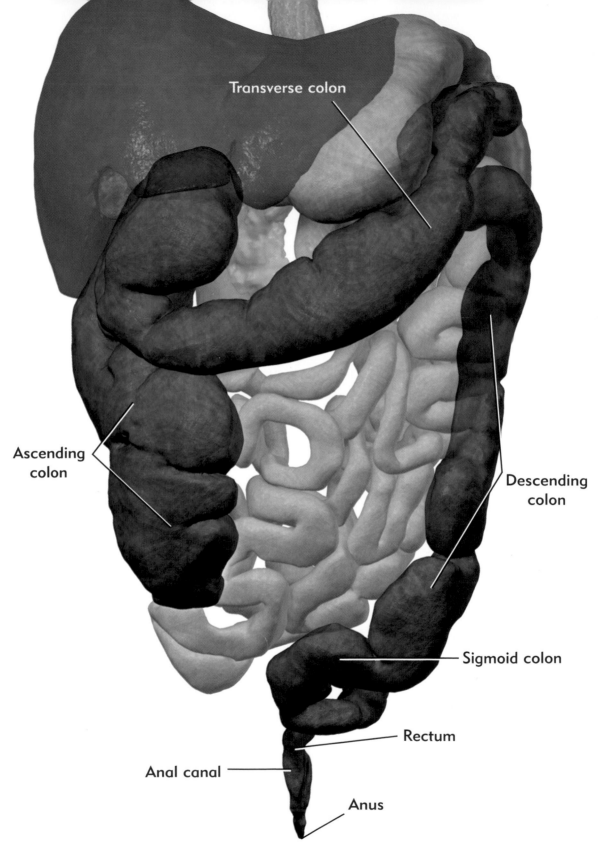

Transverse colon

Ascending colon

Descending colon

Sigmoid colon

Rectum

Anal canal

Anus

The large intestine is an average of 5 feet long and 2.5 inches in diameter. Its main purpose is to receive liquid wastes from the small intestine, absorb water and salt, and convert liquid into solid waste.

Internal Organs

The body's digestive organs are often described as a long tube. That's a good way to portray the main part of the digestive system, which includes the lower part of the esophagus, the stomach, and the intestines. But there are other parts of the digestive system and other important organs here as well. The spleen, pancreas, and gallbladder all help us to digest food. The kidneys and bladder, at the very bottom of the midsection, remove liquid waste from the body. And the liver is one of the body's most important organs, with many functions, which are discussed in chapter 4.

These organs are joined by a thick system of blood vessels. Throughout the body, arteries bring blood from the heart, and veins take it back to the heart and lungs. In general, the major veins and arteries parallel each other, though their blood flows in opposite directions.

The main artery is called the abdominal aorta. This thick superhighway for blood splits in two around the area of the navel, with each branch splitting again to provide blood to the pelvic areas and the lower limbs. The inferior vena cava is the main vein in the abdominal area, running fairly close to the aorta. Its feeder system of capillaries gathers food for cells elsewhere in the body.

THE STOMACH

Factories construct complex products from many raw materials. The digestive system is a factory in reverse. It takes complex materials and breaks them down into small pieces of raw material. It then sends these pieces along to the rest of the body to use for its energy needs and to build new tissues. The complex materials are the food we eat. The raw materials the digestive system manufactures are sugars, proteins, fats, vitamins, and other nutrients.

Digestion actually begins in the mouth, where the teeth tear food into small bits and pass them into the esophagus, a long tube connecting the mouth to the stomach. The salivary glands add saliva as a lubricant, making it easier for the food to begin its journey. Saliva also starts breaking down starches in the food. Meanwhile, the smell and taste of the food has triggered the body's digestive system, telling the stomach to get ready. Food is on the way!

Digestion can be broken into three stages. The first is preparation, where food is torn apart. This begins in the mouth and continues in the stomach. The second stage is absorption, where raw materials are absorbed into the bloodstream. This mostly takes place in the small intestine. The third stage is elimination, where unused food is collected, compacted, and passed out of the body. This takes place in the large intestine and rectum.

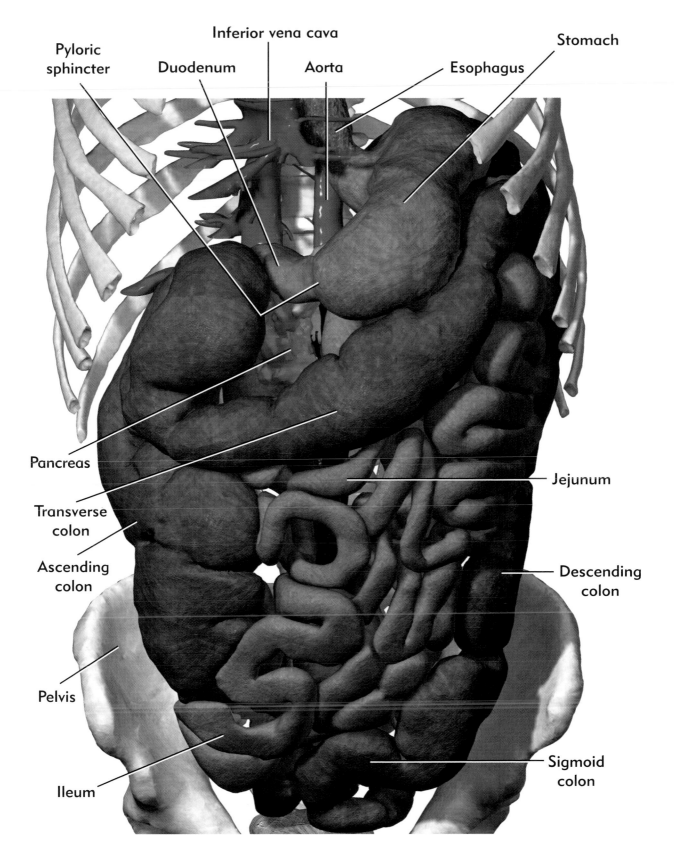

Pyloric sphincter

Duodenum

Inferior vena cava

Aorta

Esophagus

Stomach

Pancreas

Transverse colon

Ascending colon

Pelvis

Ileum

Jejunum

Descending colon

Sigmoid colon

The three-stage process of digestion takes place in the stomach, the small intestine, and the large intestine.

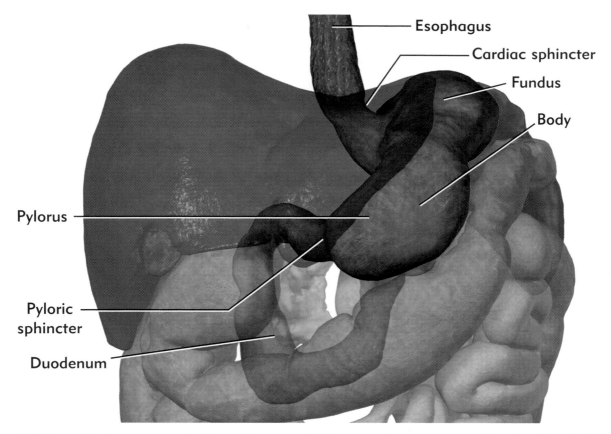

Esophagus

Cardiac sphincter

Fundus

Body

Pylorus

Pyloric sphincter

Duodenum

Although the stomach is rather small, it stretches to contain the food that we eat. It is, in fact, an expanded section of the esophagus.

As it is broken down, food becomes a watery paste known as chyme. This paste is pushed by the stomach muscles through the stomach, through its gastric canal to the pyloric sphincter, and then out to the intestines.

The Stomach

Shaped like a fat, angled J or backward C, the stomach sits just beneath the liver and toward the front of the body.

When empty, a typical adult stomach is relatively small. The hollow interior might have space for only about 50 milliliters, or 1.7 fluid ounces, barely a mouthful of soda. As a person eats, the stomach walls quickly stretch. The volume can increase to two or three liters, roughly three-fourths of a gallon of undigested food, chyme, and gastric acid. The stomach has two basic jobs: to hold food and break it into smaller bits for digestion and absorption.

Muscles

The pinkish white exterior of the stomach covers a layer of muscles. These muscles are very active during digestion. Three layers—the outer longitudinal, the middle circular, and the inner oblique—work like giant compressors. They grind food by contracting and expanding. Together, they wring the stomach and its contents like a thick, wet rag.

Looking In

Have you ever wondered what you would see if your body had a window? What if there was a doorway that would allow you to examine your internal organs? A freak injury in 1822 did just that to Alexis St. Martin, a fur trader on the United States–Canadian frontier in what is now Michigan. Shot in the side during an accident or a fight—the exact cause is unclear—St. Martin nearly died. Dr. William Beaumont managed to save him. But when St. Martin finally healed after two years, a hole remained in his side. Through the hole, Beaumont could see and touch St. Martin's lung and the inside of his stomach. The opening to the stomach had a round flap, which could be opened to observe the inside. When St. Martin was better, Beaumont conducted a number of experiments. Eventually he published a book about what he had learned.

St. Martin lived until 1880. He often spoke at medical societies, showing doctors the inside of his stomach.

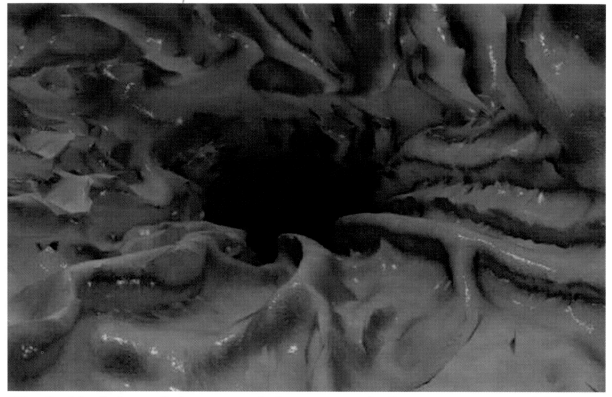

The inside lining of the stomach is composed of many rugae, or folds. These increase the surface area of the stomach.

The longitudinal muscles run from the esophagus to the pyloric sphincter like the longitudinal lines on a globe. The circular muscles run around the stomach like the equator runs around the globe. The oblique muscles look like sinewy fibers stretching from the top, or dome, of the fundus (the upper region of the stomach) downward.

The Areas of the Stomach

The stomach is divided into four different areas. From top to bottom, these are the cardia, or cardiac zone; the fundus; the body, or corpus; and the pylorus, or the pyloric part of the stomach.

The cardia includes the opening to the esophagus. A zigzag line around the interior known as the "Z line" marks the barrier between the esophagus and the stomach. Ordinarily, stomach acid is not allowed past this barrier. A powerful ring of muscles called a sphinc-ter works like a gatekeeper here. Sometimes, however, acid manages to sneak past. When that happens, the acid irritates the esophagus. We commonly call this heartburn.

The fundus is located at the top of the stomach. Shaped like a dome, it expands greatly during and immediately after a meal. It's like a reception room for food, where what we eat waits until there's room in the rest of the system.

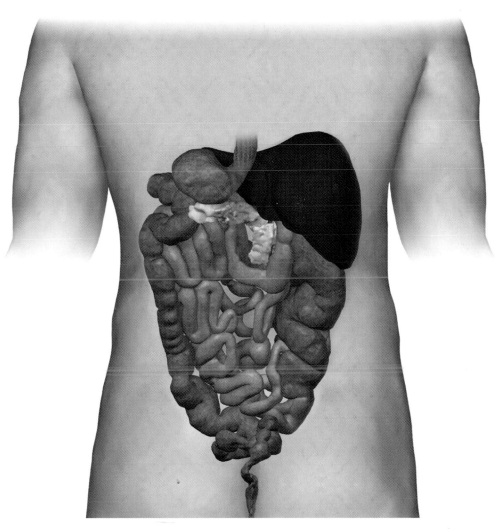

This is a posterior (rear) view of the organs of digestion and the liver. The large intestine encloses the small intestine.

Doctors call the main portion of the stomach the corpus, from the Latin word for body. This part also expands and contracts. Gastric pits line the fundus and corpus. These pits are tiny holes where the stomach juices are produced.

The fourth part of the stomach looks like a large funnel at the end of the stomach. This is called the pylorus, and it curves upward toward the duodenum, the entry to the small intestine. The point between these two organs is called the pyloric opening. Muscles on the exterior of the stomach work to allow food past the opening once the stomach is done with it. This muscle door is called the pyloric sphincter.

Acid Bath

The lining of the stomach is covered with mucous cells that protect it from gastric juice, which is mostly hydrochloric acid. Other cells have special jobs as well. Some help to produce the acid. Others can absorb nutrients easily.

The folds of the stomach are called rugae, or gastric folds. Here the gastric juices break down the food with their powerful acid. Pepsin in the juice also goes to work. An enzyme that assists chemical reactions, pepsin breaks proteins down into peptides. Peptides form the building blocks of many cells and tissues. Without them, a person can't grow or even survive.

Besides breaking down food, hydrochloric acid kills bacteria that might harm the stomach and the rest of the body. The body has several other defenses against germs that enter through the digestive tract. Lymph follicles, or nodules, lie near the stomach lining. These can target invading organisms, like bacteria, with white blood cells. The lymph system can stamp out a disease here before it gets a chance to spread.

Vomiting and Ulcers

Often when we are sick, we vomit. A series of muscle contractions force the esophageal sphincter open and compress the stomach, sending its contents upward through the esophagus and mouth. At the same time, air openings are closed, protecting our lungs.

Usually, the body uses this system to help protect itself from poisonous food. Vomiting can be caused by irritation anywhere in the gastrointestinal tract, not just the stomach.

Ulcers are a more serious stomach problem. Because of the acid in the gastric juices, the interior of the stomach is a very caustic environment. Once in a while, stomach acid burns through the protective mucous cells and attacks the stomach wall. This can create an ulcer, an open sore that causes pain and disrupts digestion. Scientists have worked for many years to discover why ulcers start. Besides an overproduction of acid, genetic factors and bacteria may help induce them. Special drugs such as cimetidine and ranitidine have been used to lower stomach acid and treat ulcers.

Stomach cancer can begin with symptoms that mimic ulcers. Like other cancers, cancer cells in the stomach stop following their normal blueprint for reproducing. They reproduce uncontrollably, crowding out healthy cells and disrupting vital functions. Stomach cancer is primarily treated by surgery. It is relatively rare in the United States when compared to the rate for lung cancer.

3
THE INTESTINES

By far the largest organs of the abdomen and the longest in the entire body, the intestines are folded within the midsection like pieces of a complicated puzzle. If they were laid out in a straight line, they would stretch the length of a school bus.

Sometimes simply called the intestine, the small intestine lies below the stomach in the pit of the midsection. Its many folds eventually connect to the large intestine, or colon. The large intestine forms a thick, over-turned U on the left side of the small intestine, connecting from the small intestine to the rectum.

The Small Intestine

The small intestine looks like a miniature fire hose folded around the midsection of the body. This tube runs about twenty-five feet in length, yet it is only about an inch wide. There are three main parts. The duodenum lies next to the stomach and is the beginning of the organ. It extends about twelve inches. Its name comes from the Latin word for twelve, duodecim.

The middle of the small intestine is called the jejunum. It runs about ten feet. The ileum is the longest part of the intestine, connecting with the colon, or large intestine.

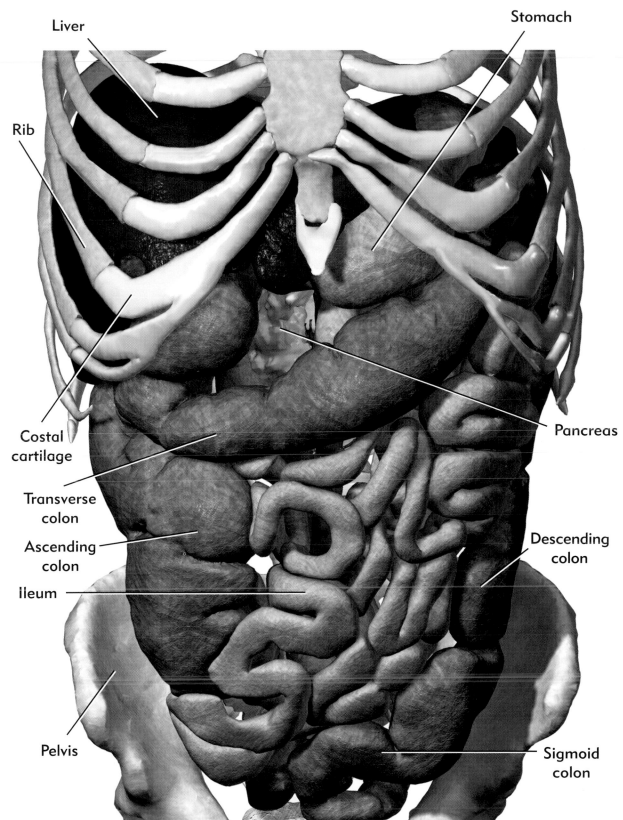

Liver

Stomach

Rib

Costal cartilage

Transverse colon

Ascending colon

Ileum

Pelvis

Pancreas

Descending colon

Sigmoid colon

The small intestine is the largest organ in the body, stretching some twenty-five feet in length. Covering its inner surface are tiny projections called villi, which further increase its surface area.

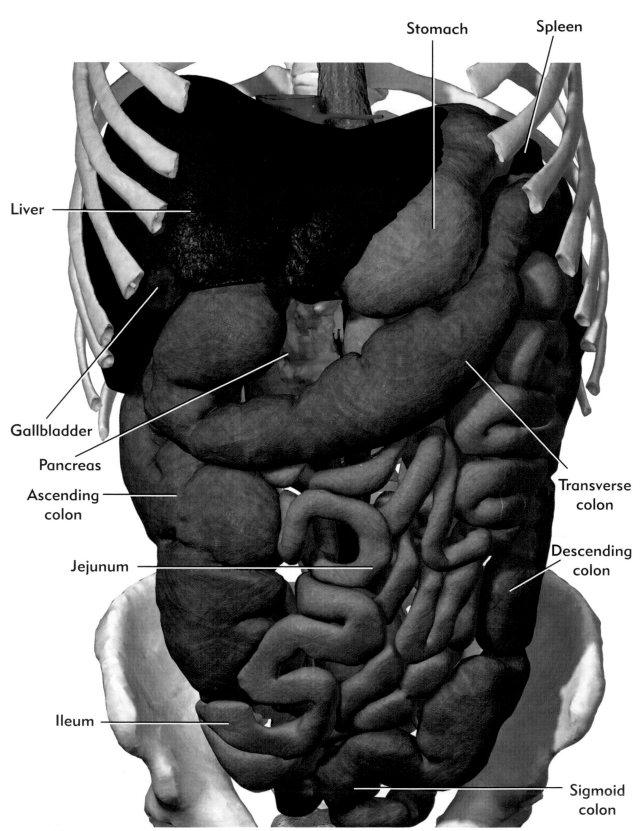

Stomach

Spleen

Liver

Gallbladder

Pancreas

Ascending colon

Jejunum

Ileum

Transverse colon

Descending colon

Sigmoid colon

Your abdomen is literally crammed with organs, including the stomach, liver, pancreas, spleen, and large and small intestines. Food has a long path to travel before it is fully digested.

Enzymes and Digestion

In the duodenum, food is mixed with an alkaline fluid from the pancreas. This neutralizes the stomach acid. Then enzymes help to further break down the food.

Enzymes in the small intestine do much of the work breaking down chyme. Enzymes are catalysts that assist chemical reactions but are not changed by them. They are large protein molecules. While in many cases chemical reactions would take place without them, enzymes help speed up the process.

A digestive enzyme called salivary amylase is injected into food in the mouth. Two more enzymes are added in the stomach, pepsin and rennin. Among the enzymes working on chyme in the small intestine are trypsin and chymotrypsin, which are both produced in the pancreas. Aminopeptidase and dipeptidase are produced in the wall of the intestine and are also vital for digesting proteins.

Complex carbohydrates are broken down with the help of pancreatic amylase, which is similar to the amylase produced by the saliva glands in the mouth. Produced in the pancreas, this enzyme does its work in the small intestine. Sugars are broken down further with the help of maltase, sucrase, and lactase, all produced in the small intestine.

Bile from the gallbladder arrives in the intestine, where it breaks fat into small droplets. Then another enzyme from the pancreas called lipase breaks the fat down further.

Intestinal Mucosa

The breakdown and absorption of nutrients takes place on the walls of the intestines, called the intestinal mucosa. This interior surface contains ridges, or folds, that look a little like a corrugated drainpipe.

The Enteric Nervous System

Do you think with your gut? A complex system of nerves lines the intestine, helping to regulate its function. In the early 1960s, Dr. Michael Gershon began studying these nerves, called the enteric nervous system. He discovered that they create an enormous amount of serotonin. In the brain, serotonin helps us to do things like learn and rest. Dr. Gershon and others discovered other brainlike chemicals in the intestine as well.

Dr. Gershon realized that the nerve system in the intestine is like a second brain. It analyzes and reacts to different situations. It sends out chemical messages to the rest of the body. It may also affect our general mood. While the enteric nervous system can't rival the brain for thinking, scientists believe further study may reveal many clues about our overall well-being. The old saying "You are what you eat" may have to be revised to "You think what you eat."

Called epithelial folds, these folds contain billions of villi, which look like fingers extending upward. Each villus has cells that have their own projections, called microvilli. This combination of folds and fingers makes the intestine's surface area massive. In fact, it's roughly 200 times as large as the surface area of the skin. Tiny blood vessels run very close to these cells to bring oxygen and ferry away nutrients.

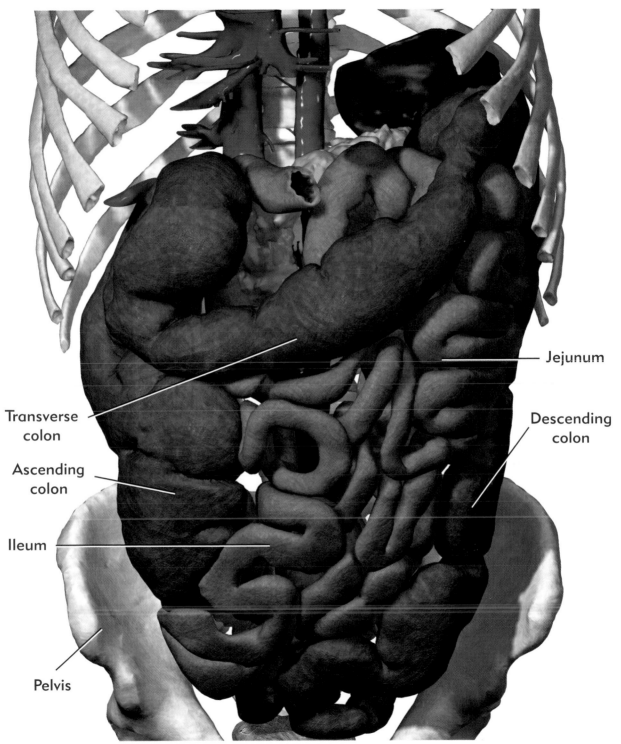

Jejunum

Transverse colon

Descending colon

Ascending colon

Ileum

Pelvis

This is a view of the intestines with the stomach removed. About two and a half pints of liquid waste enter the large intestine each day and are processed in about twelve hours.

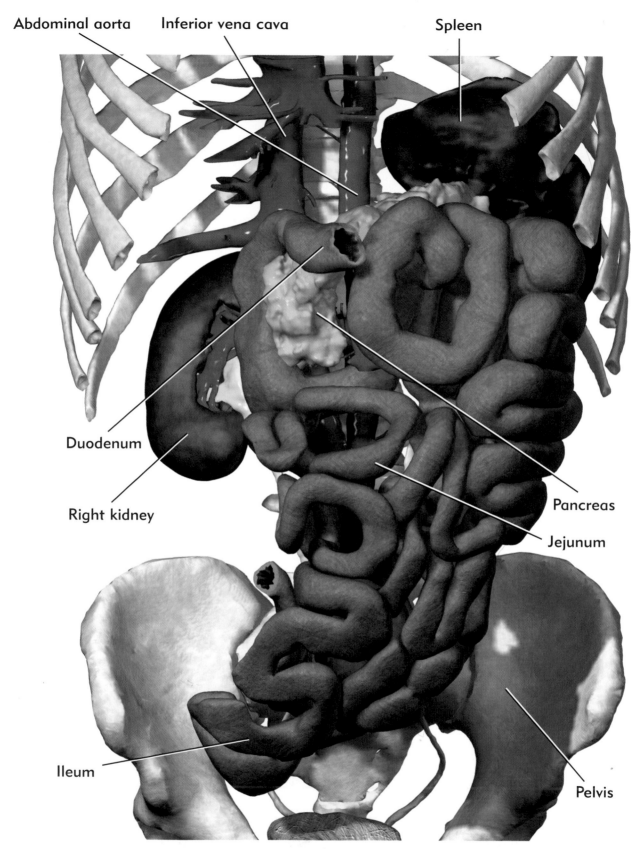

Abdominal aorta   Inferior vena cava   Spleen

Duodenum

Right kidney

Pancreas

Jejunum

Ileum

Pelvis

Shown here is the small intestine with both the stomach and the large intestine removed.

The Colon

The colon rises like an upside-down box across the inside of the midsection. It climbs on the right side to about the bottom of the stomach, crosses the body, then descends down the left side before bending back to the rectum. Doctors describe the main parts of the colon simply: the ascending colon on the right, the traverse colon across, the descending colon on the left. The descending colon leads to the sigmoid colon, which connects to the rectum. (Traverse is a fancy way of saying "to cross," which describes how the colon crosses the body. Sigmoid comes from a Greek word meaning S-shaped or curved.)

From the outside, the colon looks like a series of thick hoops or short tunnels connected together. The word "colon" comes from a Greek word for colonnade, a series of columns. The rings are formed by the bands of muscles that expand and contract as food is passed through.

Unlike the small intestine, the colon mostly absorbs water, not nutrients. As food passes through the large intestine, it becomes drier and drier. The end result is feces.

The large intestine connects to the small intestine at the bottom of the ascending colon. The large chamber near this opening is called the cecum. It can expand and contract as food is received and then passed along. At the very bottom of the cecum, generally below the connection to the small intestine, is the appendix. This small, fingerlike projection positions itself differently in different people. The appendix does not seem to have a function in digestion. It can, however, become inflamed or infected. In some cases, this can lead the appendix to rupture, causing severe pain. Doctors must remove a ruptured appendix and fight the infection, or a person could die.

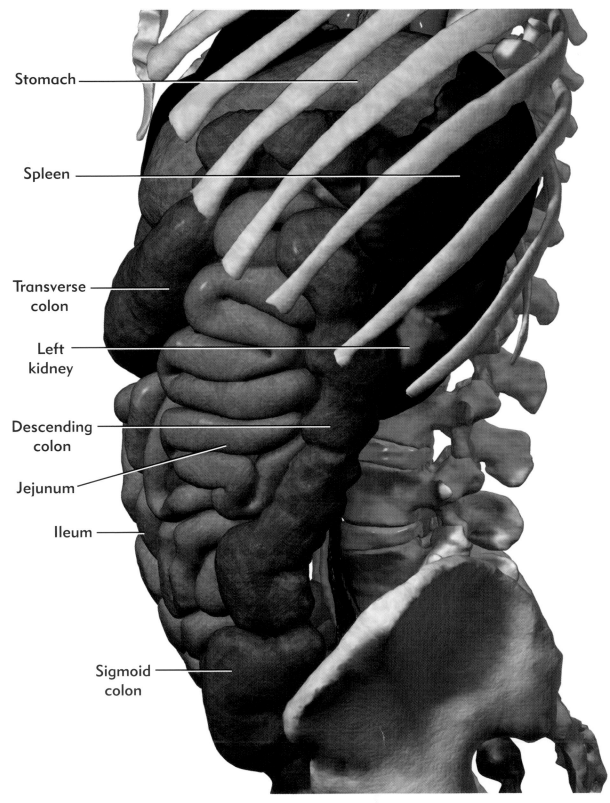

Stomach

Spleen

Transverse colon

Left kidney

Descending colon

Jejunum

Ileum

Sigmoid colon

A lateral, or side, view of the digestive organs. Only the stomach and transverse colon receive some protection from the rib cage.

Food is moved through the intestines as well as the rest of the digestive system by a series of muscle contractions called peristalsis. At each point along the way, from esophagus to rectum, the arrival of food stretches the inner layer of the organ. This pushes a layer of nerves, which in turn cause the muscles behind the food to contract. The chain reaction continues as the muscles in front of the food relax, clearing the way for the food to move forward.

Food travels through the digestive tract at a slow pace. It can take anywhere from twenty-four to seventy-two hours for it to go from the mouth to the rectum. Usually, it stays in the large intestine the longest, with an average time of about fourteen hours. Someone who is constipated, however, may have feces remain in the colon for far longer. This condition has many causes, including a diet that doesn't have enough fiber or water. Disease can also cause constipation.

Germs

Single-cell organisms called bacteria exist everywhere in the world. Many are present in the food we eat. Unfortunately, some can cause disease and death.

The stomach's acid bath kills much of the bacteria contained in food. Much of the rest ends up in the intestines, where harmful bacteria are attacked by the body's immune system. Microfold cells attract bacteria to lymphocytes, special cells where antibodies are made. The lymphocytes create antibodies, which then attack the bacteria.

In some people, the system malfunctions and the body reacts to the food itself as if it were enemy bacteria. The result is a food allergy. In most cases the reaction is mild, but severe allergies can cause death.

4
OTHER ORGANS

The stomach and intestines do most of the work of digesting food. But there are several other organs in the body's midsection, and all have important jobs. The liver, gallbladder, and pancreas manufacture chemicals important to the digestive process. The spleen and kidneys act like filters for the body, purifying it and helping to regulate the amount of water and nutrients it retains.

The Liver

The liver is the largest gland in the body. It is also rather heavy for its size. In an adult, it accounts for about one-fortieth of the body's whole weight. In a two-hundred-pound man, it could weigh as much as five pounds.

A rounded, upside-down triangle, the liver sits over the stomach. It has two lobes, or parts. The largest of these is on the right side of the body. The liver lies behind the rib cage and diaphragm, which help to protect it. The outside of the liver is smooth. It is brownish in color. The two lobes are joined on the outside by a ligament. Each lobe can work without the other.

The liver has several functions. It makes bile, which is necessary for digestion. Bile is a yellowish green liquid. If you could taste it, it would seem extremely bitter. Bile is alkaline, or the opposite of acidic. The liver passes the bile to the gallbladder, which then dispenses it to the small intestine. Bile helps the body digest fat by emulsifying it, or breaking it into small bits.

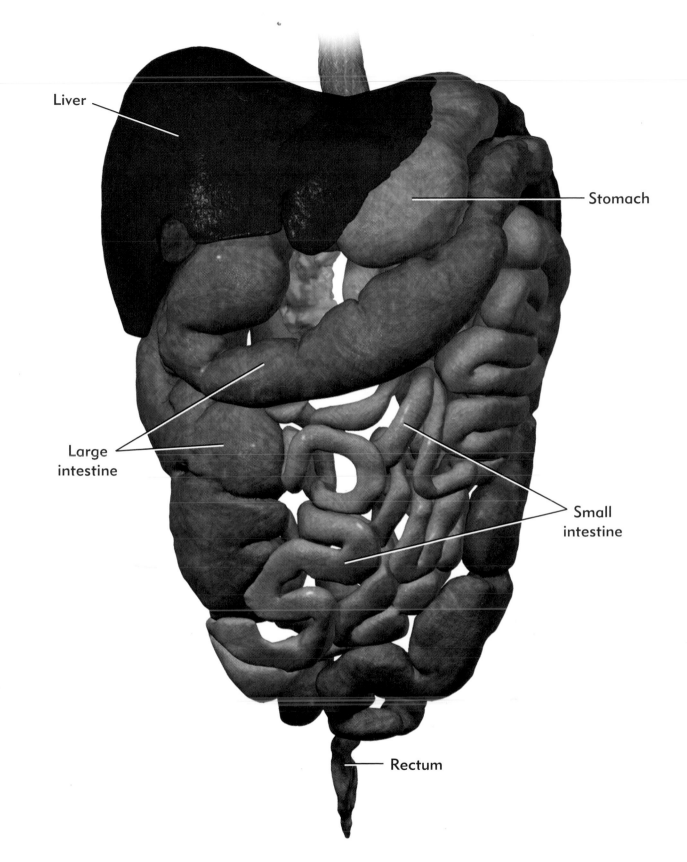

Liver

Stomach

Large
intestine

Small
intestine

Rectum

The liver, stomach, and intestines. Food moves through the stomach and
intestines by peristalsis, muscle contractions that push against these organs.

The liver also makes about a quarter of the body's lymph cells, which are used to fight disease and infection. New lymph cells enter the lymph system through lymphatic vessels, which are part of the outer layer of the organ.

The liver also helps to filter toxic materials from the blood, converting them to safer substances. Ammonia, for example, is converted to urea, which becomes urine in the kidneys. Liver cells change sugar to glycogen and help store fat and vitamins. They also synthesize blood proteins and substances such as clotting factors.

The liver cells do their work by passing blood along columns of cells that fan out from veins. This network can be easily damaged. One way is by drinking a lot of alcohol, which can cause fibers to form in the organ. These block blood vessels and disrupt the cellular architecture, preventing the cells from working right. This disease can also be caused by very poor nutrition. It is called cirrhosis.

The Gallbladder

The gallbladder looks like a green baseball tucked into the brown mitt of the liver. Ducts connect the gallbladder with the liver and the duodenum. These ducts work like the ducts or plumbing in a house. Bile from the liver flows down the hepatic ducts to the common bile duct, which is also called simply the bile duct. A sphincter, or valve, at the intestine closes the connection so that the bile backs into the gallbladder. Like a thermostat, the valve opens when bile is needed, sending the liquid in from its reservoir like hot water into a radiator.

The Pancreas

The pancreas looks a bit like an upside-down tobacco pipe, lying across the back of the abdomen. It is behind the stomach and next to

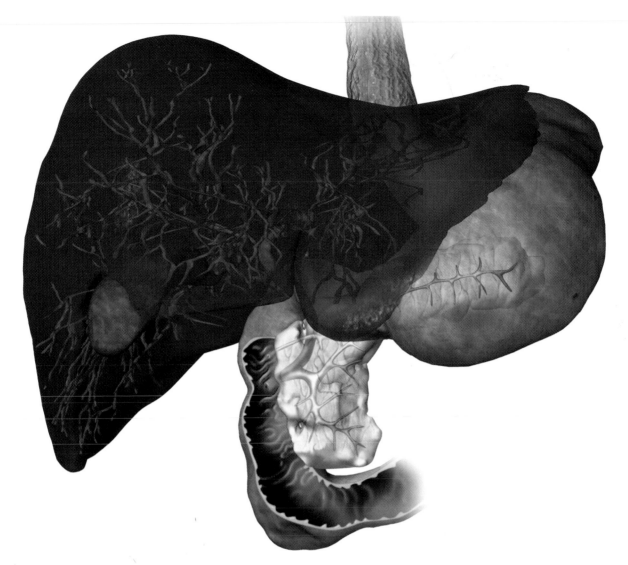

Shown here is the fine network of biliary vessels inside the liver. These vessels produce bile.

the duodenum. Part of the endocrine system, the pancreas creates a variety of hormones important to the body. Insulin is probably the best known. When the pancreas doesn't produce enough of it, a person can develop diabetes, which causes high sugar levels in the blood and disrupts the body's metabolism. The pancreas also produces glucagon, another endocrine secretion that helps the body regulate itself. These hormones enter the bloodstream through vessels that extend through the organ.

The pancreas plays an important role in digestion by making pancreatic juice. This enters the duodenum through the main and accessory pancreatic ducts at the thick part, or head, of the pancreas. This juice helps break down food in the small intestine.

The Spleen

When someone yells angrily, we sometimes say that he or she is "venting spleen." This metaphor refers to an ancient belief that the spleen stored vapors responsible for anger. Today, we know that's not true. The spleen's role is much more complex.

The outside of the spleen is purplish. It is located on the left side of the body, behind the stomach. While the size and specific shape of the spleen varies from person to person, you can get a good idea of the organ's appearance by clenching your fist. Part of the lymph system, the spleen protects the body against infection. Its job is to filter foreign substances and worn-out components from the blood. It's also a reservoir, an emergency holding tank for serious bleeding.

Blood flows into the spleen from the splenic artery and through a network of small blood vessels. The spleen filters the blood, returning it to the circulatory system through the splenic vein.

The Kidneys and Urinary Tract

As it is digested, food passes through the stomach and intestines and is eventually released through the rectum as feces. Individual cells of the body expel their own waste products into the bloodstream.

These wastes, along with excess water and salts, flow through the blood to the kidneys. Shaped like large beans, the kidneys lie toward the back at the bottom of the abdomen just above the hip. The lower two rungs of the rib cage protect most of the kidneys.

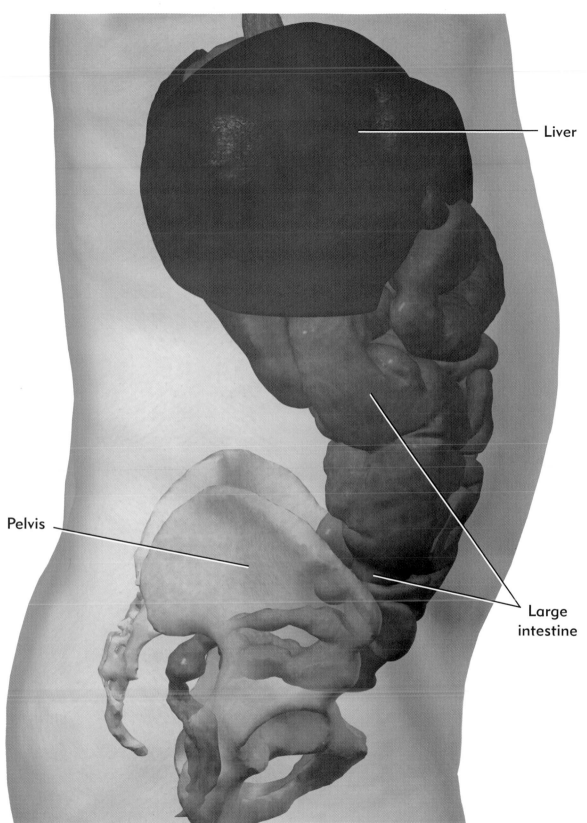

Liver

Pelvis

Large
intestine

The location of the digestive organs within the abdomen. When the
abdominal muscles are not exercised and become flabby, a person is said
to have a "pot belly."

The kidneys are like large filters, processing the blood that arrives from the aorta through a number of renal arteries. ("Renal" comes from the Latin word for kidney.) About 1.3 liters of blood, or about the amount in a medium-sized soda bottle, flow through the kidneys each minute. In an adult, 170 liters of water and liquid waste can be expelled by the kidneys in an average day.

The liquid filtered out from the blood drains as urine. It flows down the ureters from each kidney to the bladder in the pelvis. The ureters are more than simply tubes. They reabsorb parts of the urine, mix it with their own secretions, and return it to the body for different functions. The rest reaches the bladder, where it collects and is then expelled.

The Adrenal Glands

If you've ever needed a burst of energy during a race, you called on your adrenal glands. These glands lie at the top of each kidney, next to the lower part of the diaphragm. They are also called suprarenal glands because they're on top (supra) of the kidneys, or renal organs. Adrenaline is actually only one of the many hormones these glands produce. Also called epinephrine, adrenaline is joined by norepinephrine to increase heart rate and blood pressure when exercising hard or when the body must be alert. Corticosteroids and androgens cause the kidneys and other organs to retain sodium and water during stress, which increases blood pressure. With their different hormones, the adrenal glands help to regulate a variety of body functions, especially during times of stress.

Overall, the body's midsection might be compared to a small factory. The complex process of digestion takes place here. Other vital functions are controlled or influenced by the organs housed in the trunk. It may be called the stomach in everyday conversation, but it is much more than one digestive organ.

GLOSSARY

artery   Major blood vessel that carries blood from the heart to other organs of the body.

capillary   Small blood vessel that connects with an artery or vein.

chyme   Liquid paste of food created during the early stages of digestion in the stomach.

constipation   Retaining feces in the colon longer than normal. Elimination of feces varies greatly from person to person, and it can range from twenty-four to seventy-two hours after eating.

digestion   Process of turning food into usable raw materials for cells.

endocrine system   Those body systems that manufacture hormones to regulate the body's function. Major endocrine glands include the pancreas and the suprarenal glands. Other glands include the pineal gland, the hypothalamic nuclei, the pituitary, the thyroid, and the parathyroids. The male testes and the female ovaries are also part of the system.

enzyme   Special protein that acts as a catalyst in the body. Catalysts are not changed by chemical reactions, but they are able to speed them up.

heartburn   Burning feeling in the middle of the chest. Usually this is caused by stomach acid leaking upward into the esophagus. It does not actually involve the heart.

hormone   Chemical substance produced by the body's endocrine glands. A hormone can have a short-term effect, such as helping you to run from a threatening situation. It can also have a long-term effect, such as helping to increase muscle growth.

indigestion   General term usually used by people to describe pain or discomfort after eating. There are many possible causes, such as spicy food, food allergies, stress, and illnesses.

lipid   Fat or fatlike substance. These necessary compounds are insoluble in water, presenting a special challenge for the digestive system.

mucous   Special secretion that lines and protects the stomach from gastric acid.

pepsin   Enzyme that breaks proteins down into peptides in the stomach.

rugae   Folds in the interior part of the stomach.

ulcers   Holes in the stomach or other parts of the digestive system. Quite painful, they disrupt digestion and can be deadly if not treated.

vein   Major blood vessel that carries blood back to the heart.

vitamins   Wide range of organic chemicals necessary in small amounts for body functions.

vomiting   Emptying of the stomach contents through the esophagus.

FOR MORE INFORMATION

Gray's Anatomy Online
Web site: http://www.bartleby.com/107
An online version of *Gray's Anatomy*, a classic anatomy text. The text is very advanced, but the illustrations are easy to understand and give a good idea of the position of various organs.

The Human Body
Web site: http://library.thinkquest.org/28807/data/home.htm
Student-produced site with overviews of different body systems, including the digestive tract.

The Mad Scientist Library
Web site: http://www.madsci.org/libs/index.html
Index for anatomy section of a large science site.

FOR FURTHER READING

Bryan, Jenny. *Digestion: The Digestive System.* New York: Dillon Press, 1993.

Clayman, Charles B. *The Human Body: An Illustrated Guide to Its Structure, Function, and Disorders.* New York: Dorling Kindersley Publishers, 1995.

Collins, Barbara J. *Exploring and Understanding the Human Body.* Westchester, IL: Benefic Press, 1971.

Elting, Mary. *The Macmillan Book of the Human Body.* New York: Aladdin Books (Collier Macmillan), 1986.

Epstein, Sam, and Beryl Epstein. *Dr. Beaumont and the Man with the Hole in His Stomach.* New York: Coward, McCann & Geoghegan Inc., 1978.

Goldsmith, Ilse. *Anatomy for Children.* New York: Sterling Publishing Co., 1964.

Jackson, Gordon, and Philip Whitfield. *Digestion: Fueling the System.* New York: Torstar Books, 1984.

Kapit, Wynn, and Lawrence M. Elson. *The Anatomy Coloring Book.* 3rd ed. San Francisco, CA: Benjamin Cummings, 2001.

Parker, Steve. *Digestion.* Brookfield, CT: Copper Beech Books, 1997.

INDEX

About the Author

James Toriello has written more than twenty books for children and young adults.

Photo Credits

All digital images courtesy of Visible Productions, by arrangement with Anatographica, LLC.

Series Design

Claudia Carlson

Layout

Tahara Hasan